Deadlines Amuse Me!

Poetry by

Steffani Ballard

Presentation by *BookLeaf Publishing*

Web: www.bookleafpub.com

E-mail: info@bookleafpub.com

ISBN: 9789357440196

First edition 2023

To the one who taught me that life is short and unpredictable, and time is precious and nearly never perfect; always shoot your shot no matter how scared you may be because second chances don't always come back around.

To my best friend forever. No take backs. I love you to the moon and back, to infinity and beyond. Even then. Even still. Even now. I always will.

You are my sunshine.

Thank you for always believing in me.

This is for you,

Alie Rose

1 Corinthians 13

ACKNOWLEDGEMENTS

Big thanks and much love to all of those throughout my life who have supported and encouraged me in my writing.

You know who you are.

PREFACE

Hopefully this book doesn't stink…

Wafting In

Pen to paper.
I have nothing to write.
I have not written in quite some time.
And yet, in that same time,
I have felt everything so deeply;
I have seen the worst this life can give;
I have heard the cries of loved ones taken;
I have screamed at the top of my lungs to survive;
I have tasted the bitter end.
And all the while, I have not written.
No air to feed my flame.
So now, I'll take this time that I've been given
to tear open the wounds of a soul left rank and rotting;
I'll jot down some words on these pages,
creating something for once other than destruction.
Pen to paper.
I have so much to write.
I have not written so much in so little time.

Mise-en-scène

Abstract paintings from contract artists
cause obstruction and erosion of the mind.
Every observation through squinting eyes
like looking through the holes in the walls
to see the naked ladies dancing
under the stars that they claim
have a gravitational pull –
a force that pulls them together
to collide with that certain someone
who lights up your galaxy
like the burst of a massive supernova.
Energy converts to energy.
Nothing is created; nothing is destroyed,
and yet, we destroy ourselves
trying to create a better work of art,
like the *Mona Lisa* or Edvard Munch's *The Scream* –
that piercing cry, as from pain or fear,
supported by the diaphragm
as if singing out loud with passion,
burning like a fire, admitting heat;
thermal energy pulsating through every limb,
relinquished by every fingertip,
extinguished by every word filled with disdain,
filled with hate and heated conviction.
These words that we hide in our hearts

that we might not sin against God,
yet the tips of our tongues spit venom
like a snake – that serpent that taunted Eve,
who taunted Adam
with the mouthwatering, erotic taste
of the forbidden fruit.
And with just one bite,
just one shaking hand of the one
clenching that sacred brush,
with just one ill-made stroke of paint,
DaVinci's *Last Supper* becomes distorted,
and Van Gogh's *Starry Night*
may as well have been
just a lunar eclipse.

Nature vs. Nurture

In Cowen, West Virginia, the morning breeze
rushes through the trees, rustling
the dead leaves to the ground. The wind
whistles past each fragile limb
like the breath of God whispering,
"Now, go." Dew drops dance upon
petals, leaves and branches, rising
into the heavens as the sun rises in the East.
It peeks over the peaks of the mountains,
light pouring out over the land, trickling
through the treetops, warming and waking
the living. A Mourning Dove blasts through the thicket,
booming like a shotgun firing. A white-tailed deer
sprints off into the distance, chased
by the aggravated crowing of a buzzard.
The woodpecker laughs out loud, while song birds
sing back and forth the same tune sung
in different tones, some high and some low.

Back in Huntington, she sits behind the Jomie Jazz
Center, listening to the bending vibrations
of a steel guitar seeping out from under
the backstage doors. The accompaniment of
a grand piano stumbles in from behind. A battle
begins between melody and harmony, jazzy riffs

and classical trills. The tangle of sound thrills
her unsound heart. She reads
the finger-printed message in the scum
on the wall, "Fight war, not wars.
Destroy power, not people."

No one sleeps at night. Everyone sleeps
through the day to play in the twilight.
Upon waking, we dance beneath the stars,
we sway in the moonlight. We lose
ourselves, we lose control. A night
shining dark, as cold as a motionless heart,
we move in it. We move to the silenced beats
of our souls. Wide awake, the living dead
move their bodies, unattached.
And the moon tilts its head and smiles.

In the city, she sits at a bus stop, her heart
drowning in her stomach. People pass.
Cars drive by. Nobody sees her. Nobody
stops. Everyone keeps running, like the
rushing water in the nearby Ohio
hours after a hard rain.

In the mountains, leaves stained red
fall to the earth. They gather
at the foot of a suffering tree,
a Red Oak being stripped barren
in a season of death. The wind

is no more. The land is calm.
Not a creature stirs.
Not a single bird
carries a tune.

And with no place to go,
we sit all alone
and hope for a home.

Day Care

After saving animals from erupting volcanoes and watching movies on oversized cardboard bricks that doubled as pillows, I set out the lunches and assisted the rowdy boys and chatty girls in the bathroom as they washed the recess residue from their pint-sized hands. Cameron, only four, waited impatiently in line to use the potty, dancing in place with a grimace or grin (I couldn't decide) on his face. Only one more before him, but he just couldn't hold it. Relieving the urge, he spilled out, "I love you!" His accident flooded my chest cavity, leaving a mess too vast to tidy.

Later that day, I sat on the colorfully carpeted floor with toddlers teeter-tottering all around as nursery rhymes sounded in the background. Two tiny boys, Liam and Colin, plopped down by my side, playing with the beads on my bracelet. Watching in wonder, I noticed my sleeve pulled up, exposing my unlovely truth. Reacting too late to conceal my shame, I felt their precious fingers smooth over the scarred surface of my forearm. Looking up at me, Liam pointed at my wounds and called, "Boo-boo! Boo-boo!" Colin responded, grabbing my hand to touch the same surface, lean down, and kiss the pain away. His gentle touch stung my flesh, flooding the mess in my chest as my eyes welled up.

And at the end of the day, I'm made to wonder how such small vessels can hold so much when the bigger ones always seem to burst.

To Your Inner Child

Come with me to a place I know
where there's joy and excitement,
and on adventures we can go;
where Peter Pan and Captain Hook
play shipboard games
in a babbling brook.
You too could join me
and the crew,
and laugh and joke
like the pirates do.

Off to Neverland!
That's where *I*'ll be
to never grow up,
to live life by the sea
with mermaids, Indians,
and a Lost Boy or two,
to live a life of happiness.
Oh won't you come too?

All you need to get there
is a little faith and trust,
a childlike heart and the magic
from a pinch of pixie dust.
With imagination galore,

we can fly, we can fly,
we can take off and soar
out to that second start on the right
and then straight on 'til morning.
Come with me now with no delay.
Consider *this* your warning:

Though age is a number forever progressing,
growing up is a choice you make;
and if you decide to stop all believing,
growing up is the risk you take.

In the Orchard of Eden

That time you took me apple picking –
an experience I had not yet had
in my adult life, only a childhood memory
that escapes me now – you took me
to the prohibited row
of produce not to be picked;
you pulled up your dress
and revealed to me
the most beautiful apples,
straight for the tree of Eve.

But you were always more
of a Lilith, weren't you?

And, oh my God, in that moment,
I wanted nothing more
than to sink my serpent teeth
into your forbidden fruit
and taste your pulp
on my slithering tongue.

Zodiac

Alas, I am a Gem!
An air sign.
To be grounded
is to be flying –
soaring
high amongst the clouds,
dancing with the stars,
high enough
up above
to gently kiss
the moon.

> Don't be surprised
> if I make you swoon;
> my charm is undeniable.
> But understand,
> my other side
> is equally despisable.

So flip the coin.
Pick your poison.
Who knows
what happens next.

I could be your
superhero,
or I could be your
cause of death.

Salvation

Come with me
on this hot summer night
to the church parking lot,
where I'll take you to Heaven
on our way straight to Hell.

A Storm of Passion

Your hands on my body.
Electricity piercing my skin.
Shocked.
Scorched by your lightning.
Now,
Pouring in sweat
from head to toe,
high winds rush through my mind.
The sound of your moan
floods my ears.
The boom of your thunder
makes my heart pound
in my chest,
as I pound
into you
over and over.
Harder.
Faster.
Steadily splashing
into your puddles.

Dirty Hippie Huffing

The Pheromones mingling
with deep, sweet Patchouli.
Notes of Vanilla
swirled in Lavender.
Fields of Champa Flower,
Oakmoss and Sandalwood
drunk in Bourbon and Bergamot:
Peace of Mind;
perhaps *Obsession*;
maybe a *Classic Match*.
Right Guard –
right choice.
Lasting freshness
in through the nose
out through the mouth.
Spice of life –
fragrant impression.

Meaningless Music

Like the lyrics to a catchy song,
you run through my mind, nonstop.
You're stuck there, playing over and over
like a broken, vile record...

I just can't get you outta my head...

Last night you held me and I was stuck
in your melodic stare and harmonious hold.
You strummed the chords of my heart
on my back. Those pleasant notes linger...

Every night, every day, just to be there in your arms...

What's happening here? Between us,
is there anything? Or am I just singing
in the shower, no one else around to hear it?
Could you be captivated by this tune...

Won't you stay...

Lost Love

Live.
Laugh.
Laugh until you cry.
Cry until you can't breathe.
Breathe until you've reached that state of calm.
Calming rest.
Deep sleep.
Death.

Grief

If a tree falls in the woods,
and no one is around to hear it,
does it make a sound?

If I say I love you,
but you're not around to hear it,
does it lose its meaning?

The feeling is real,
but the expression
is silenced.

How hard it is to be heard
when no one can hear
over the silenced expressions
overcrowding their minds.

How loud it must be
for the one
left speechless.

Isle of John Donne

It comes in waves –
   that empty feeling,
     submerging,
       dragging you down.
        You gasp for air,
      inhaling the salty sea
    as you drown.
   A suffocating experience
enough to kill you.
   That is unless
     you're fit to fight,
       to keep swimming,
        resurface,
       break through the ocean's barrier,
    push to reach the shore,
   and walk once more
upon desert land.

Last Call

Sitting alone at my coffee bar,
enjoying a few shots of espresso,
I decide to give her a call.

Today is her birthday –
eighty-three years young.

She tells me how my mom always
says I love you before she goes.
"It's nice," Granny says.

I tell her about how when I was a child
I wouldn't go to bed unless
the last thing said was,
"Good night, I love you."

She asks if I still do that.
I say, "Yeah, I think I do."

She says to me, "That's good, ya know?
You never know when
it will be the last time
you get the chance
to tell them."

I look at your photo
hung up on my wall,
finish off my drink,
sigh and say,
"I know."

All too well,
I know.

Ticking Away

It's too cold to sit outside,
so I sit in silence.

Time moves so slow,
as if not even moving at all.

It's like God dumped a bucket of paint on the world,
and said, "Behold, thou shall watch it dry!"

Have you ever felt too empty to cry?

I want to beat my head off the wall
until the sound reverberates
back into my chest,
and kick-starts my heart.

Why is it so hard some days
to just get up and start
to do anything at all?

Just breathing sometimes feels too heavy.

I dropped my blank stares on the floor,
so I sat backwards on the couch,
and said, "I'm just bored."

I'm fine.
I'm just tired.
It's been a long day.

I didn't get out of bed
this afternoon until
half passed three.
Glancing now
at the clock,
and it reads 5:30.

I'll be damned.

I thought it was later than that.

Looking up, I wonder
what's new on the ceiling.

It's too dark to look out the window,
so I'll leave the curtains drawn.

Daily Routine

Every morning, I wake up,
and turn on my espresso machine,
glance up to your photo,
and tell you, "Good morning."

Coffee for Two was the title
of the poem you wrote me –
one of many that I still have.
I read it as I brew, and remember
just how you like your coffee –
"Hazelnut. Sweet, yet strong."

I cried the day we tucked you in.
(A continuation from the moment
I heard you had gone to rest.)
I kissed your forehead, sending
kisses to your soul, and shared
one last laugh with you
over how pissed you would have been
over the shape your eyebrows were in.
I held your hand as I laid our picture
in bed beside you.

I drove myself home as
I tried to drive away the pain.
Drunk upon arrival, I kept going –
a shot for you,
a shot for me,
until Whiskey was calling the shots
and I was lying on the floor,
adorned in crimson and remorse,
wondering why I wasn't asleep
in bed beside you.

Now, every day,
I brew my espresso –
a doubleshot for you,
a doubleshot for me.
I make my coffee –
Sweet, yet strong.

Just for today, every day,
I say my prayers,
and count my steps,
glance up to your photo,
and remember you –
your loving memory
kisses my forehead,
keeping me awake.

Cheap Thrills

I went shopping today.
My local Goodwill greeted me
as I walked in.
I wasn't looking for anything
in particular;
yet I perused the aisles
aimfully.

I stumbled upon a number
of admirable suitors,
but the change in my pocket
assured me that
the timing was all wrong.
Reluctantly, many desirables
were put back in proper places
with the notion,
"If you're here when I come back,
it was meant to be."

I didn't leave empty-handed.
My novelties included:
an oversized scarf,
an old man's sweater,
and a satchel to hold
my pens and journal.

All for only seventeen dollars.
What a steal!

I spent only a dollar more
at the grocery store next door –
my dinner
for probably
the next week and a half.

Thrift shops are the remedy
on my bad days.
I never know what I may find.
They say money
can't buy happiness,
nor love,
but sometimes
just a two dollar treasure
is enough to make me smile
and fill the void.

Just for today,
my heart is warm
wrapped in a scarf
and another man's sweater.

Sunshine

I love the way she turns the clouds pink, swirling
in the blue – creating cotton candy skies.
Oh how sweet! Traces of purple sweeping
overhead, lingering in her light. Her beauty –
divine. Her warmth is like a hug. She smiles
from above. Her rays point the way, and
every day she leads us to rise up and shine.
Every day made new by her luminous design.

Face the Music

Listen to that rhythmic sound,
that internal beat so smooth,
that noise inside your head so thrilling;
feel that urge to bust a move.
Get that intoxicating impulse
to just break free
from the world as you know it,
separate from reality.
Create your own steps,
and make it what you will.
Fill your soul with joy,
and always keep it real.
Fast or slow –
the tempo is up to you.
Do whatever keeps you groovin',
whatever makes you *you*.
Forget about observers;
forget what they may say.
Just do what makes you happy,
and do it each and every day.
There will never be a consequence
if you never take a chance.
So give up the funk, my dude;
this life is but a dance.

Ascending: 13 Going on 30

*"The top of one mountain is always
the bottom of another."*

        –Marianne Williamson

There I stood, just a girl – half child, half teen,
thirteen, and it was all downhill from there.

Starting to roll, impersonating a pencil,
I was more like a log, thick and round,
hitting every bump and divot on my way
down with no hope of slowing, of getting back up.

When my roll became a tumble, I knew I had lost
control. While falling hand over foot, as awkward as
I was, the hill bruised my body from head to toe, so I
scarred my arms from hand to elbow, trying to match
the pain felt by my battered frame, trying to make a
road of speed bumps to slow me down, as if the
knocks from the knoll weren't enough already.

There were times when I would turn over and twist
so I could glimpse the peak of the hill where smiles
bloomed in the sun and laughter fluttered in the
wind, and for a second I was still.

If I could just reach that place above me...

The tossing continued as I was hurled over backwards,
sick with motion, the urge growing
as I began to shrink. Always big enough before
to realize I would never be adequate,
I became small enough to purge away more
than just the benders. I became bent in blindness.

But when I finally hit rock bottom, crashing hard
at the foot of the hill, I was still.

My bruises slowly began to heal as I looked up to
see where the sun was shining, and I began to climb
up the speed bump rungs I had finished
on the downfall. And though there were still
bumps and divots to hike over, I ascended to the top
with my head wide open and my eyes held high.

Here I stand, just a woman – still healing, still worthy,
now thirty, and it is all uphill from here.

Buried Alive

Perfection never rests,
and neither shall I.
Like a diamond,
I come alive under pressure.
Unearthed and polished,
I shall be
forever.